PROFIT

the **Real Truth** *about what it is, where it comes from, how it improves the quality of life for everyone*

is not a four-letter word

PR⬤FIT

is not a four-letter word

the Real Truth *about what it is, where it comes from, how it improves the quality of life for everyone*

JOHN A. STIEBER

Illustrations by Tom Clare

AMACOM
American Management Association International

New York • Atlanta • Boston • Chicago • Kansas City • San Francisco • Washington, D.C.
Brussels • Mexico City • Tokyo • Toronto

This publication is designed to provide accurate and authoritative
information in regard to the subject matter covered. It is sold
with the understanding that the publisher is not engaged in
rendering legal, accounting, or other professional service. If
legal advice or other expert assistance is required, the services
of a competent professional person should be sought.

Library of Congress Cataloging-in-Publication Data

Stieber, John.

Profit is not a four-letter word: the real truth about—what it is,
where it comes from, how it improves the quality of life for
everyone/John A. Stieber.
        p. cm.
    Includes index.
    ISBN 0-8144-7983-9
    1. Profit   2. Markets   3. Quality of life.   I. Title.
HB01.S693 1998
658. 15'5—dc21   97–32858
                                                     CIP

Printing number

10 9 8 7 6 5 4 3 2 1

For Tonni

Contents

Foreword ....*xi*

My Background ....*xiii*

The First Cup of Coffee in the Morning:
  Brought to You by the Pursuit of Profit....1

The Tax Man Cometh: Our Public
  Goods and Services Depend on Profit......3

The Fable of the Tailor....................................5

The Way People Usually
  Talk About Profit.......................................7

What We Were Never Told in
  School About the Human
  Behavior That Leads to Profit....................9

Checking the Scoreboard:
  Profit as Information.................................11

The Rules of the Game:
  Rule Number One....................................13

The Rules of the Game:
  Rule Number Two....................................15

Why We Never Stop Consuming 17

The Rules of the Game:
  Rule Number Three.................................19

$$$

A "Sidebar" About the
   Rules of the Game..................................21

Profit, Scarce Resources, and Survival........23

The Four Horsemen of Production..............25

Accounting vs. Economic Profit:
   Like the Tailor Says, "The
   'Bottom Line' Doesn't Tell
   the Whole Story" 27

Fixed Costs Are Sunk Costs........................29

Variable Costs Are Changeable..................31

Shoes vs. Socks: Opportunity Costs 33

Farmer Jones: More About
   Opportunity Costs..................................35

From the Farm to the City..........................39

The Mother of All Costs:
   Opportunity Costs..................................41

A Closer Look at Accounting Profit............43

A Closer Look at Economic Profit 45

The Only Way to Define Profit..................47

The Criticism of Profit..............................49

Profit Isn't "Good" or "Bad"—
   It's an Event 51

Another Kind of Event or
   Happening 53

$$$

Profit That Is Acquired Illegally 55

One More Comment About Illegal Profit..57

The Difference Between the
Event Profit and
the Pursuit of Profit 59

Once Upon a Time I Pursued Profit............61

Profit vs. Profit Maximization 63

A Lecture by a Well-Intentioned
Scientist 65

Opportunity Costs and the
Late, Great Planet Earth 67

What Is Profit Maximization? *or*
If Profit Maximization Is Not
Merely Making the Bottom
Line as Large as Possible, Then
What Is It? 69

The Technical Definition of Profit
Maximization 71

How Marginal Revenue Works:
A Mini Lecture 73

How Marginal Cost Works:
Another Mini Lecture 75

The Real World of
Profit Maximization 77

The Behavior That Maximizes Profit 79

$$$

Profit Maximization and
    the Bottom Line 81

Profit Maximization and Ethics 83

Profit Comparisons: One of the
    Least Important Uses of the
    Concept of Profit 85

Afterword...87

Index 89

$$$

Foreword

I am writing this little book with an impassioned hope that those who read it will develop a better understanding and appreciation of the role of profit in our daily lives. If I am successful, then the credit belongs to all of those men and women who have ever had to concern themselves with the allocation of scarce resources. If I am unsuccessful, then the failure is mine.

$$$

My Background

I am an economist. For the last three decades, I have been teaching as a full-time faculty member in the school of business at a private university located in the southwestern region of the United States. I have taught undergraduate BBAs, full-time MBAs, part-time MBAs, and executive MBAs. I have also conducted seminars for the executives of several major U.S. and foreign corporations.

These students range in age from twenty to fifty-plus. They have come from every state in the union and just about every continent in the world.

The BBAs usually have no business experience. The full-time and part-time MBAs usually have a level of business experience associated with middle managers. The executive MBAs and the seminar participants have extensive business experience. One of the executive MBAs is currently the chief executive officer of a Fortune 1000 company, and another recently retired as the chief executive officer of a Fortune 1000 company. There are others who are the chief executive officers of smaller companies.

Every time I teach a new group of students, I have some expectations about their understanding of the basic tenets of business. What I get is a mixed bag. Some exceed my expectations. Most fall short.

There is, however, one concept all of them recognize, but few, if any, truly comprehend. I am talking about the concept of profit.

Most students and managers think about profit as a residual after costs are subtracted from revenues (sales). This perception is a generally accepted but simplistic description of profit. Only a few of them have engaged in any serious contemplation about the very special human behavior that results in profit. Fewer yet are aware of the benefits from the behavior of pursuing profit for people—*all people.*

PROFIT

the Real Truth *about what it is, where it comes from, how it improves the quality of life for everyone*

is not a four-letter word

The First Cup of Coffee in the Morning: Brought to You by the Pursuit of Profit

*D*escribing the benefits that accrue from the pursuit of profit is not an easy task, because they are so obvious that we usually take them for granted. When our clock radios wake us in the morning to our favorite music mixed with reports about traffic conditions and the weather, we drag ourselves out of bed in our central-heated and air-conditioned homes and take *hot* showers. We then sit down with coffee that was automatically brewed when the clock radio turned on, eat precooked breakfasts that were prepared in microwave ovens, and read newspapers that were hand-

$$$

delivered to our homes. We finally put on our clothes, get into our cars, and drive to work on expressways that cost hundreds of millions of dollars to build.

I'll bet a dollar to a penny that most of us have never interrupted our cycle of living and acknowledged, even for a moment, that the quality of our lives is directly related to the pursuit of profit. *We just take these blessings for granted.*

I remember a student in one of my classes who asked me to be more specific about the benefits we receive from the pursuit of profit. In response to his request, I asked him to look around the classroom, his home, and his community. I pointed out that they wouldn't exist if it were not for the pursuit of profit. I also told him that public goods and services such as our streets, highways, county hospitals, public universities, police protection, fire protection, and national defense all owe their existence to, you guessed it, the pursuit of profit. To this day, I don't believe he has gotten the message.

The Tax Man Cometh: Our Public Goods and Services Depend on Profit

*T*he notion that the goods and services provided by the public sector are the result of the pursuit of profit is usually a bit difficult to accept, but their origins are the same as the goods and services provided by the private sector. Here's why.

We are a people of government, and our government, like all governments since the beginning of time, collects revenue. The

YOUR TAX DOLLARS AT WORK

$$$

source of this revenue is as predictable as death. Governments tax the wages, rents, interest, and profits that are paid by businesses to the factors of production (resources) they hire. And so it is that business, while producing goods and services in the private sector, also generates the income that governments tax to produce the public goods and services the community wants.

The Fable of the Tailor

There was once an immigrant tailor who came to this country and opened up a shop. He sewed on buttons, stitched hems, made suits, and did all those other things that tailors do. One day his son, who was an accountant, dropped by for a visit. While he was there, he noticed two cigar boxes sitting next to the cash register. One was labeled "paid bills," and the other was labeled "unpaid bills." The son chastised his father for keeping his records in such an unprofessional manner because the old man didn't know what his profit was.

UNPAID | PAID

The father lovingly put his arm around the shoulders of his son and told him that when he came to this country many years ago, the only possessions he had were his clothes. Now he

$$$

had a home, a car, a good business, good health, a daughter who was a college professor, a daughter who was an engineer, and a son who was not too sharp as an accountant. The old tailor then said, "When I add up all of my blessings and subtract the clothes on my back, what remains is my profit."

This story was told many years ago in a homily given by Monsignor Raphael Kamel, the pastor of All Saints Church in Dallas, Texas. The message is simple, yet powerful. It is also unusual. Unlike most stories that describe profit as ill-gotten or abusive, this one talks about profit in terms of human achievement and social good.

The Way People Usually Talk About Profit

*U*sually, when people talk about profit, they do so within a technical framework. The technical definition of profit was created by business to identify what remains after costs are deducted from revenues (sales).

Essentially, this definition defines profit as a residual that can be positive, or negative. When the residual is positive we identify it as a profit. When the residual is negative, we identify it as a loss.

The technical definition of profit is totally impersonal. Revenues enter the profit equation as a positive number, but they tell us nothing about the energy, the effort, the discipline, and the commitment of the people who produce these revenues for their companies. Costs enter the profit equation as a negative

$$$

number, and they also tell us nothing about the human creativity, the personal skills, the attention to detail, and the quality of labor of the people who generate these expenses.

If we really want to capture the essence of profit, then we must move beyond any technical definition. We have to discuss profit in terms of human behavior, because the making of profit is a human endeavor.

What We Were
Never Told in School
About the
Human Behavior
That
Leads to Profit

*T*he behavioral component of profit calls attention to the manner in which people acquire it. Profit is earned through a very special kind of human behavior. It is the behavior of people producing the goods and services the community wants and needs, such as health care, schools for our children, food for our tables, and shelter for our families.

By any measure, this kind of behavior constitutes the highest level of human activity and the highest level of social good. It is people engaged in business who provide the goods and services the community needs, not those $$$

in the arts, in the news media, or in politics.

For any business to create profit, it must engage in highly disciplined people activities. In many ways, this activity is like the activity of producing a great symphony, a well-written play, a fine painting, a vintage wine, a piece of sculptured glass, or a new scientific discovery. It demands excellence, delivers quality, and requires an abundance of creativity. In fact, the best businesspeople are more often than not the most creative.

Moreover, I believe that some of the greatest works of art in this world are the American farm, IBM, American Airlines, a Boeing 747, an Apple computer, a Ford Mustang, and the neighborhood grocery store. For a comprehensive list of these works of art in your community, just look in the yellow pages of your local telephone directory.

Checking the Scoreboard: Profit as Information

*E*very morning before they go to work, millions of people, mostly guys, open up the sports page and check the scoreboard to see how their favorite baseball, football, basketball, or hockey team performed. If their team scored more points than the opposition, without looking at the statistics, they can predict with high probabilities that their team outperformed the opposition in runs, pitching, fielding, pass completions, number of baskets, and so on. In other words, just by looking at the score, millions of people have a lot of information about their teams.

And so it is with profit. As an information parameter, profit is one of the best barometers businesses have to rank the things consumers want. If there is more profit in producing personal computers than there is in producing calculators, then consumers are telling business that they want the one more than the other. Accordingly, businesses will shift their resources to comply with this ranking, and they will make more computers and fewer calculators.

Profit, or lack of it, is also a signal for businesses to enter or exit the marketplace. For example, from 1973 through 1980, when profit was high in the oil industry, there was a surge of entry by new companies. Since then, profit in the industry has declined, and a large number of companies have gone out of business.

The Rules of the Game: Rule Number One

I f we are to understand the role of profit in our lives, then it is important for us to know the *rules of the game.* These rules, which are imposed upon us by the marketplace, are often referred to as tenets. We don't have to be acquainted with every tenet of the marketplace, but we do need to address those that are essential to our discussion.

When Adam and Eve lived inside the Gar-

$$$

den of Eden, they had unlimited resources. That is why they had everything they wanted except the fruit from the Tree of Knowledge of Good and Evil, which they were forbidden to eat. What they discovered when they were cast out of the Garden was that their resources were suddenly limited. They could no longer have everything they wanted. Furthermore, they had to provide for themselves by the sweat of their brows.

In addition to the anthropological, historical, and religious significance associated with this eviction, these ancient writings call attention to what is perhaps the most consequential tenet of the marketplace: We, the descendants of Adam and Eve, now live in a world of *scarce resources*. And, in such an environment, we can never, ever have everything we want.

The Rules of the Game: Rule Number Two

O ne could argue that if our wants as a species were less than the available resources that exist outside the Garden, then the consequences of scarce resources would be negated. Fortunately or unfortunately, depending on one's perspective, we seem to be born with an insatiable desire to consume. I remember a colleague who once said that if the universe were finite, Homo sapiens would devour it before the black holes in space got their chance.

From the moment we are conceived until the moment we die, we never stop consuming. Our appetite for goods and services is relentless. Even after death, many of us continue to consume. We use the services of lawyers, accountants, and other professional people to distribute our wealth or manage our assets so

$$$

that the income can be used to support our children, charities, or whatever other beneficiary we may designate.

This insatiable appetite of ours brings us to the second tenet of the marketplace that is important for our analysis of profit: With the introduction of Homo sapiens to this planet, we must now contend with a world of *infinite wants*.

Why
We Never Stop
Consuming

A human being is an organism that must have certain things to continue to survive and function. For example, without food we would starve. In certain parts of the world, without clothing and shelter we would freeze. Without water we would die.

Over time, people satisfy their hunger with different kinds of foods (wants). Today they $$$

eat a steak. Tomorrow they eat pasta. The same thing holds true for clothing. When people go country-and-western dancing, they wear jeans and boots. When they go to work, they wear suits, dresses, and shoes.

Wants also arise because of cultural influences. In most communities, high levels of consumption, such as having a house, a car, a megascreen television, or a college degree give people status. So, people often acquire these things to get status.

New wants occur while we are satisfying old wants. When we first began to cook our food, we used an open fire. This cooking ritual created a want for a brick oven, followed by a stove, then a microwave oven; only the future knows what the next cooking technology will be.

The Rules of the Game: Rule Number Three

*C*ombining scarce resources with infinite wants brings us to our third and final tenet: *More is better than less.* Whenever this tenet is postulated, people usually ask, "More of what is better than less of what?" The answer is: *More goods and services from a given set of resources is better than fewer goods and services from the same set of resources.*

In the jargon of the business manager: this tenet would be stipulated in the following manner. The efficient use of scarce resources is better than the inefficient use of scarce resources. The measure of efficiency in this case would be more goods and services from a given set of resources, rather than fewer goods and services. Obviously, I am not referring to illegal goods and services.

$$$

A "Sidebar" About the Rules of the Game

*T*he word "marketplace" means different things to different people. I am using it as a synonym for private enterprise.

Private enterprise has some unique property rights associated with it. Not only do individuals have property rights (ownership) over the goods and services they purchase; they also have property rights (ownership) over the resources they purchase to produce the goods and services the community wants.

In the United States, we take this ownership of resources for granted. Until recently, people in the socialist countries of the former Soviet Union and Eastern Europe were excluded from the ownership of certain resources used in the production of goods and services. The property rights associated with these resources belonged to the state.

$$$

Profit,
Scarce Resources, and
Survival

Given the quality of life we enjoy today compared to that of those who lived before us, it is easy to forget that the efficient allocation of scarce resources is a very serious matter. In fact, it is imperative for our survival. The history of mankind from ancient to modern times is full of examples of the suffering and death people have endured because of the misallocation of scarce resources. I submit that much of the massive starvation we have experienced around the world during my lifetime is directly related to the misallocation of scarce resources.

The institution that concerns itself with the efficient allocation of scarce resources is business. The engine that drives the allocation process is profit. And the fuel used by this engine is the pursuit of profit.

Profit and the efficient allocation of scarce resources are not mutually exclusive. They are two sides of the same coin. In fact, I would even go so far as to say that they are synonymous. Without profit, there is no incentive to allocate resources efficiently. If businesspeople do not allocate scarce resources efficiently, there will not be any profit. Therefore, if the efficient allocation of scarce resources is imperative for our survival, so is profit.

In those economic systems where profit was removed from the resource allocation equation, the results have been disastrous. Look at what happened to Eastern Europe and the Soviet Union. Food crops rotted in the fields while store shelves and human stomachs stayed empty because no profit motivation existed to fill these shelves and stomachs. All of these countries are now acknowledging that profit is a politically acceptable dimension to the efficient allocation of scarce resources.

The
Four Horsemen of
Production

I have already used the word "resources" more often than the word "profit." It is time for these resources to step up and identify themselves.

Whenever an individual starts a business, the end product or service will require a mix of four basic resources or factors of production. I like to refer to them as the four horsemen of production.

The first resource is land, and the payment that is made to bring land into the productive process is called rent. The second resource is capital, and the payment that is made to bring capital into the productive process is called interest. The third resource is labor-time, and the payment that is made to bring labor-time into the productive process is called wages. The fourth resource is the entrepreneurial and creative skills of people, and the payment that is made to bring these skills into the productive process is called profit.

For those of us who like our life less complicated, there is another definition. Anything used in the production of goods and services is a resource.

Accounting
vs.
Economic Profit:
Like the Tailor Says,
"The 'Bottom Line'
Doesn't Tell
the Whole Story"

*I*f we were to ask most managers, including business owners, for a simple statement of accounting profit, they would probably tell us that accounting profit is equal to total revenue minus total cost. Total cost is commonly arranged into total fixed cost and total variable cost.

Economic profit can also be written as total revenue minus total cost. But, from an economic perspective, total cost is arranged into total fixed cost, total variable cost, and opportunity cost.

$$$

The only reason accountants do not include opportunity cost in their model is that they are forbidden to do so by statutory mandate. They are as knowledgeable about opportunity cost as economists. However, as recorders of the company's previous business activities (historians), they are forbidden by law to include opportunity cost as a cost of doing business.

Fixed Costs Are Sunk Costs

*T*otal fixed costs are those costs that do not change when you produce goods and services. They include land, buildings, and equipment, such as computers.

If you were to build a manufacturing plant that had the capacity to produce a hundred widgets over the life of the plant, the cost of that plant would be the same whether you produce nothing, fifty widgets, or one hundred

$$$

widgets. Hence the expression "fixed costs."
Businesspeople often refer to fixed costs as
sunk costs because, once the plant is built,
your money is sunk into the plant.

Variable Costs Are Changeable

*T*otal variable costs are those costs that do change or vary when you produce goods and services. They include such things as labor-time and materials.

Unlike fixed costs, if you build a widget plant and you produce nothing, you won't buy any labor-time and materials, so you will have zero variable costs. If you were to produce ten widgets, you would buy a certain amount of labor-time and materials, so you would then have some variable costs. If you were to pro-duce more widgets, you would purchase more labor-time and materials, so you would have more variable costs. As output either increases or decreases (varies), you use more or less labor-time and materials. That is how we get the expression "variable costs."

$$\$\$\$$$

Shoes vs. Socks: Opportunity Costs

O pportunity costs are the goods and services that won't be produced from a given set of resources because these resources were used to produce some other goods and services. The operative word here is *other*.

When you live in a world where there are not enough resources to produce everything that everyone wants, then all resources have competing alternatives or other uses. If a given set of resources is used to produce shoes, then it can never be used to produce socks. The opportunity cost for the community, once these resources are used to produce shoes, is the socks or other goods and services that can never be produced by these same resources.

Farmer Jones: More About Opportunity Costs

*W*hen I was a teenager, I went to a private high school located along Lake Erie in the northwest corner of the commonwealth of Pennsylvania. To help pay for my tuition, I worked part time on a farm.

I remember that every spring, the manager of the farm, whom I will call Farmer Jones, struggled with the same problem. He had five hundred acres of good planting land, a large herd of milking cows, some marginal acreage to pasture his cows, and some hogs.

The soil was a sandy loam, and it had a lot of small rocks in it. He used to say that given the climate and the sandy loam soil of the area, he could grow only potatoes and feed-corn. Potatoes were his cash crop. Corn was his winter feed for his livestock.

$$$

Farmer Jones was very aware that every acre planted in corn could not be planted in potatoes. He knew that his planting acreage was a scarce resource. He also knew that his opportunity cost for planting potatoes was less corn and that for planting corn was fewer potatoes.

I can assure you that Farmer Jones did not drive around the county telling people that he had just planted five hundred acres of corn and, because we live in a world of scarce resources, his decision had created an

opportunity cost equal to the five hundred acres of potatoes that would not be grown on this land. He internalized this cost into the operation of his farm in the following manner.

He would sit down at his desk in front of his hand-operated "adding machine" and do what he called some planning (simulations). He would forecast a series of prices for a bushel of potatoes, his cash crop, and for a bushel of corn, his feed corn. He would then estimate how much cash he would give up if he planted more feedcorn. He would also estimate how much more his feedcorn would cost him if he planted more potatoes because he would have to buy some of it from other farmers or feed companies.

What he was calculating was the opportunity cost associated with planting more corn than potatoes and that for planting more potatoes than corn. He wasn't aware of it, but his whole planting operation was driven by his opportunity cost.

I'll bet a dollar against a dime that if Farmer Jones were alive today, he would do the same $$$

kind of analysis. The only difference might be that he would do his planning (simulations) on a computer instead of on an "adding machine."

From the Farm to the City

We now know how Farmer Jones used opportunity cost to make his planting decisions. But what about his city cousin, who was in the manufacturing business? Did he do things differently? Let's find out.

I have a friend who is the chief financial officer of a megasized manufacturing company. This company has factories located in different towns and cities throughout the United States. It also has production facilities in other countries.

While fishing for big-mouth bass several years ago, I asked my friend how his company decided what products to produce and what products not to produce. His response was very informative.

He told me that, like General Motors or the $$$

corner doughnut shop, his company had a limited amount of resources at its disposal (our legacy from Adam and Eve). He also said that his company was making a pretax rate of return of no less than 14 percent on all existing products it was manufacturing. He referred to this 14 percent as an internal rate of return or target rate of return.

He went on to say that any manager who wanted to introduce a new product for manufacture had to demonstrate that the project would yield a rate of return equal to or greater than 14 percent. If he or she couldn't, the project was rejected because it would be an inefficient allocation of the company's resources.

Like Farmer Jones, when this company was comparing rates of return between new products and existing products, it was calculating the opportunity cost associated with using resources to produce product "a" versus product "b" or "c." And, like the planting decisions of Farmer Jones, the manufacturing operation of this company was driven by its opportunity cost.

$$$

The Mother of All Costs: Opportunity Costs

*I*n a world of infinite wants and scarce resources, even though we talk about fixed and variable costs, there is only one cost that businesses ever incur. You guessed it: *opportunity cost*. Let's see why.

Remember our friend Farmer Jones? When he decided to produce corn on his land, he couldn't produce potatoes. His opportunity cost was the forgone potatoes.

What happens if Farmer Jones buys a new tractor? A tractor is one of those fixed costs about which we spoke earlier. Once Farmer Jones uses his money to buy a tractor, he cannot use this same money to buy a combine. Farmer Jones has just incurred an opportunity cost, the forgone combine.

Suppose Farmer Jones spends his money on fertilizer. Fertilizer is a variable cost. Once

$$$

Farmer Jones spends his money on fertilizer, he cannot spend this same money on insecticides. Farmer Jones has just incurred an opportunity cost, the forgone insecticides.

The bottom line of this discussion is that every time a business uses any resources, fixed or variable, it incurs opportunity costs.

A Closer Look at Accounting Profit

*F*rom our discussion of accounting versus economic profit, we know that accounting profit equals total revenue minus total fixed cost and total variable cost.

According to this model, whenever revenues exceed fixed and variable costs, accounting profit will be positive. Most businesspeople refer to such situations as cases where the company is profitable.

If fixed and variable costs exceed revenues, accounting profit is negative. Most businesspeople refer to such situations as cases where the company is losing money.

If fixed and variable costs are equal to rev-

$$\textbf{PROFIT} = \begin{smallmatrix}TOTAL\\REVENUE\end{smallmatrix} - \left(\begin{smallmatrix}TOTAL\\FIXED\\COST\end{smallmatrix} + \begin{smallmatrix}TOTAL\\VARIABLE\\COST\end{smallmatrix} \right)$$

$$$

enues, accounting profit is zero. Most businesspeople refer to such situations as cases where the company is breaking even.

Whereas this model can tell us whether accounting profits are positive, negative, or zero, it cannot tell us anything about the opportunity cost associated with these accounting profits because of the alternative use of the resources involved. To do this, we have to revisit economic profit.

A Closer Look at Economic Profit

*E*conomic profit equals total revenue minus total fixed cost, total variable cost, and opportunity cost.

The only difference between the accounting model of profit and the economic model of profit is opportunity cost. In fact, we could say that economic profit is equal to accounting profit minus opportunity cost.

Whenever economic profit is equal to zero, this model tells us that the business is making accounting profit but that its opportunity cost is equal to its accounting profit. Economists refer to this situation as a case where economic profit is equal to the company's opportunity cost.

$$\text{ECONOMIC PROFIT} = \text{ACCOUNTING PROFIT} - \text{OPPORTUNITY COST}$$

$$$

Whenever economic profit is positive, the company is making so much accounting profit that it more than covers the opportunity cost of the company. Economists refer to this situation as a case where economic profit is greater than opportunity cost.

Whenever economic profit is negative, there are three possible events. One, the company is making negative accounting profit and cannot cover any of its opportunity cost. Two, the company is making zero accounting profit and cannot cover any of its opportunity cost. And three, the company is making positive accounting profit, but not enough to cover all of its opportunity cost. Economists refer to these three situations as cases where economic profit is less than opportunity cost. Most managers relate only to accounting profit. The world would be better served if all managers related to economic profit and the alternative uses (opportunity cost) associated with the resources at their disposal.

The Only Way to Define Profit

*A*t the beginning of this book, I pointed out that we live in a world of scarce resources and infinite wants. I also noted that one of the important postulates of the marketplace is that more goods and services from a given set of resources are better than less.

There is only one way to be certain that we are getting the most out of a given set of resources. We have to examine alternative uses for those resources. In other words, we have to find out what it is we are giving up (the forgone goods and services). And, as we already know, any time we look at alternative uses for our resources, we are taking stock of our opportunity cost.

Remember Farmer Jones? Remember the chief financial officer? Both of their businesses *$$$*

were driven by alternative uses of their resources (their opportunity cost). Both of them were looking beyond their accounting profit to their economic profit. And what did they learn by doing this?

Whenever a company's profit more than covers its opportunity cost, there are *no* other more productive uses for its resources. It is using its resources efficiently. The same holds true when profit is equal to opportunity cost. Whenever profit does not cover opportunity cost, there are more productive uses for the resources. The company is not using its resources efficiently.

Now you know why economists describe profit as being equal to, greater than, or less than opportunity cost. Any other description of profit begs the question of efficiency and ignores the issue of scarce resources.

The Criticism of Profit

*U*nfortunately, profit is criticized much more than it is acclaimed. It has been the whipping-boy of politicians, the print media, television newscasters and personalities, self-appointed speakers for labor and consumers, environmentalists, the arts community, and the religious community. All of these groups, at one time or another, have joined in a chorus of righteous indignation opposing the profit of "big oil," "big banks," or "big corporations."

The problem is that most of this opposition $$$

has more to do with demagoguery, political posturing, and fund-raising than it does with rational economic analysis.   Many of these groups are against all profit except their own.

Profit Isn't "Good" or "Bad"— It's an Event

*T*he reasons for criticizing profit are many and varied, but the underlying cause is that few people, including those who are in the business of pursuing profit, truly understand what a positive impact it has on all of us. Too often we tend to look at profit as being inherently good or inherently bad, when, in fact, it is neither.

Profit is an event, a happening. As we already know, it can only be equal to, greater than, or less than opportunity cost. What is good or bad about profit is *how* we as human beings acquire it. For example, if we acquire profit by selling illegal drugs, that is bad. If we acquire profit by producing legal drugs that relieve suffering, cure diseases, and extend life, that is good.

I cannot help but think about people like $$$

Ross Perot and Bill Gates. In the pursuit of profit, these men have created employment opportunities that have enhanced the quality of life for more than a hundred thousand men and women in communities all over the world. These jobs provide food, clothing, housing, health care, education, recreation, and more for themselves and for several hundred thousand family members. For the life of me, I just don't understand why this kind of behavior is considered by some to be inherently bad. I'm convinced that the benefits for people from the pursuit of profit are absolutely, positively, inherently good. I am also convinced that it takes a colossal amount of arrogance to ignore these benefits.

Another Kind of Event or Happening

*D*uring the decade of the 1980s, there were two friends who were musicians. I will refer to them as Frick and Frack.

One day Frick invited Frack over to his "pad" to listen to a song that he had just composed. It was a beautiful ballad that lingered in Frack's memory.

When Frack returned to her home, she recorded the song on a tape, acquired a copyright, and sent the tape to a recording studio. Six weeks later, the song rose to the top of the recording charts.

You don't have to be a rocket scientist to realize that the song was stolen by Frack. Furthermore, her behavior was illegal. Maybe her *$$$*

behavior was criminal. Be that as it may, the event or happening from this illegal behavior was that the song was published. That doesn't make the song illegal. The behavior that led to its release was illegal.

If Frick had copyrighted and recorded the song, the event or happening would have been the same—the song would have been published. That wouldn't have made the song legal. The behavior that led to its release would have been legal.

And so it is with profit. The behavior that leads to the event or happening we call profit can be legal. Or the behavior that leads to the event or happening we call profit can be illegal. But, regardless of the behavior that produces profit, the event or happening we refer to as profit can *only be* equal to, greater than, or less than opportunity cost.

Profit
That Is Acquired
Illegally

One of the major problems people have with profit arises from the practice of some individuals of using their business in an illegal manner. This kind of human behavior is commonly referred to as *profiteering*. Webster's Dictionary defines profiteering as the act of making what is considered an unreasonable profit, especially on the sale of essential goods, during an emergency. Journalists have extended this definition to include illegal business practices.

Webster's definition has no substance in the body of historical and contemporary microeconomics. As I have previously explained, economic profit can be equal to, greater than, or less than opportunity cost. Any other description requires a value judgment on the part of the individual asserting the description. $$$

For example, when Webster's Dictionary talks about making an *unreasonable* profit, the adjective "unreasonable" is a value judgment on the part of the publisher that begs the question of efficiency and ignores the issue of scarce resources.

Illegal business practices that are erroneously tagged "profiteering" cannot be dismissed like Webster's definition, because these are criminal acts that have a basis in statutory law. However, one could ask if it is fair to put the label "profiteer" on people who engage in illegal business practices and not put a label on those engaged in other types of illegal activities. Why not establish a special label for all individuals who use their positions or professions to break the law? Then we could call lawyers who do this kind of thing, "lawyer-teers"; men of the cloth, "religiteers"; news media people, "mediateers"; film makers-"movieteers"; actors and actresses, "artis-teers"; and environmentalists, "environmental-iteers." Better yet, why not call all people who break the law, regardless of how they do it, *$$$* *criminals*?

One More Comment About Illegal Profit

*V*ery often it is business that is labeled a profiteer. Business is not a monolithic institution with its corporate office located in some large municipality, making decisions without people. Business is only a word to describe a certain kind of people behavior. Business is people. Consequently, if a company is engaged in any illegal activity, it is the people within the company who are committing a crime.

$$$

As a group, businesspeople are no better and no worse than any other group of people, including physicians, educators, and religious leaders. The company that makes a profit does so, among other things, because the people working for it are operating within the law. The act of making a profit is perfectly legal. It is criminal when a company makes a profit by violating the law.

The Difference Between the Event Profit and the Pursuit of Profit

O n more than one occasion, I have said that profit is an event, a happening. I have also said that people acquire profit by producing the goods and services the community wants. I refer to this acquiring process as the pursuit of profit.

When people pursue profit, they get involved in two kinds of behavior. First, they try to produce a product or a service (which is behavior/action). Second, they try to generate revenues by selling their product or service (which is behavior/action). There is no other kind of business activity. Businesspeople are involved in sales activities and/or production activities. *There are no profit activities.*

At the end of the month, the quarter, the

year, all of this sales and production activity leads to an event or happening. That event or happening is profit, and profit can only be equal to, greater than, or less than opportunity cost. It cannot be anything else.

These sales and production activities, which are human activities, can be good, bad, reasonable, unreasonable, legal, illegal, or any other descriptive label you want to put on them. But the result of this activity, irrespective of the kind of behavior involved, is profit. Profit is not a human activity. The pursuit of profit is a human activity. Again, profit cannot be good or bad. Only the behavior involved in the pursuit of profit can be good or bad.

Once Upon a Time I Pursued Profit

Many years ago, I settled down in a large city located in what is called the Deep South. Instead of going to work for some company, I purchased a custard stand. The closest thing to it in existence today is a Dairy Queen.

Seven days a week, I opened up my business at ten in the morning and closed it at ten in the evening. During those hours, I made and sold custard (ice milk), purchased supplies, hired and trained people, ran radio ads, cleaned all my equipment, and more. I did all the things I had to do in that business because I was pursuing profit.

Throughout that year I was involved in either production activities or sales activities. $$$

But no matter how hard I worked or how many hours I stayed at the business, I never found any *direct* profit activities. What I discovered very quickly was that pursuing profit was where all the action was. Profit happened because of the things I *did* in the pursuit of profit.

At the end of my first year in business, I lost money. Stated another way, I made negative accounting as well as negative economic profit. So I sold the business and went to college.

Profit
vs.
Profit Maximization

*W*e have already said that accounting profit is equal to total revenue minus total fixed cost and total variable cost. Economic profit is equal to accounting profit minus opportunity cost. We also know that profit, whether accounting profit or economic profit, is an event or happening that occurs when people engage in those kinds of human activities that generate revenues and produce goods and services.

Profit maximization is a different kind of animal. Most men and women in business probably think of it as maximizing their bottom line or accounting profit. Essentially, this perception is an accounting perspective. It is not an economic perspective. And it is not the meaning of profit maximization.

There are those who believe that profit

maximization implies that companies can and will do anything to make the most profit they can, regardless of the means. They accuse business of raping the land, polluting the environment, destroying our institutions, and so on. This perspective on profit maximization is usually advanced by those who have never run a business.

A Lecture by a Well-Intentioned Scientist

*A*bout ten years ago, a faculty member from one of the science departments attended a business school faculty meeting at the university where I was working. He asked to address our group and proceeded to berate us for teaching our students to maximize the bottom line (accounting profit) by using business strategies that were destroying the planet Earth.

He accused us of teaching students that, in the interest of profit, it was good business to pollute our rivers and streams, foul our air, contaminate the soil, and destroy the ozone layer. The shocking part of his diatribe was that he believed what he was saying.

At the time, I thought to myself that the arrogance and conceit of this well-intentioned, grossly ignorant man were reprehensible. He $$$

had never attended a single lecture by any professor in the school of business. He *assumed* that my colleagues and I were teaching this kind of drivel. His conclusions were based on anecdotal data about a few businesspeople, out of tens of millions, who were abusing the system.

Opportunity Costs and the Late, Great Planet Earth

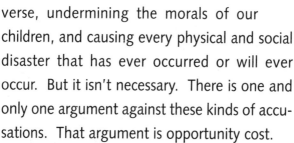

I could write a book shooting holes in the arguments about how business, by maximizing its bottom line or accounting profit, is destroying the universe, undermining the morals of our children, and causing every physical and social disaster that has ever occurred or will ever occur. But it isn't necessary. There is one and only one argument against these kinds of accusations. That argument is opportunity cost.

I cannot help but think about the biblical reproach that asks, "What does it profit a man if he gain the whole world but suffer the loss of his soul?" Within this context I would like to ask, "What does it profit a company if its opportunity cost exceeds its bottom line?"

Companies that are rational when it comes to making business decisions have absolutely no incentive to engage in strategies to maximize their bottom lines by destroying the Earth. The opportunity cost associated with such a decision would be cataclysmic. And what are these cataclysmic opportunity costs for businesses? They would destroy their resource base and their customer base, thereby destroying themselves. And that, my dear Watson, is the ultimate opportunity cost any company can incur.

$$$

What Is Profit Maximization?

or

If Profit Maximization Is Not Merely Making the Bottom Line as Large as Possible, Then What Is It?

*A*ny analysis of profit maximization begins and ends with the people who are involved in business. What is it that these people do? They engage in the human behavior of allocating the scarce resources that produce the goods and services the community wants. Stated another way, businesspeople are resource allocators. That is their profession; that is their mandate.

There is a directive that comes with this $$$

responsibility of being a resource allocator. Businesspeople must allocate scarce resources *efficiently*! And how do businesspeople allocate scarce resources efficiently? They do it by adhering to the principles inherent in profit maximization, also referred to as profit maximizing.

Rather than concentrating on the bottom line, profit maximization focuses on the *behavior* that leads directly to bottom-line profits and losses. Rather than concentrating on numbers, profit maximization focuses on all of those human activities that generate these numbers.

When I use the phrase "profit maximization" or "profit maximizing," I am referring to everything and anything that goes into good business. Stated another way, profit maximization refers to everything that goes into converting scarce resources into what people want and doing it efficiently.

The Technical Definition of Profit Maximization

*F*rom a technical perspective, profit maximization is defined as the set of conditions in which marginal revenue is equal to marginal cost and the marginal-cost curve intersects the marginal-revenue curve from below. At this point, and only this point, the company is operating at a level of efficiency that guarantees the community the maximum amount of goods and services that can be produced from a given set of scarce resources. These efficiencies are usually calculated mathematically and are rarely translated into behavior.

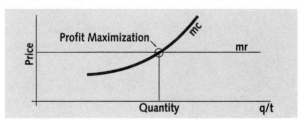

How Marginal Revenue Works: A Mini Lecture

*M*arginal revenue is defined as the additional revenue received by the company from an additional unit of sales. Suppose that Company X, which does business in a highly competitive market, has sold eight widgets at ten dollars each. The revenues received by Company X are equal to eight units times ten dollars, or eighty dollars.

Suppose Company X now sells another widget for ten dollars. The revenues are now equal to nine units times ten dollars, or ninety dollars.

The additional revenue the company receives from selling an additional widget is ten

MARGINAL REVENUE IS
→ **ADDITIONAL REVENUE**
→ **FROM AN**
→ **ADDITIONAL UNIT OF SALES**

$$$

dollars. Since marginal revenue is defined as the additional revenue from an additional unit of sales, ten dollars is the marginal revenue Company X receives by increasing its sales from eight widgets to nine widgets.

How Marginal Cost Works: Another Mini Lecture

Marginal cost is defined as the additional cost incurred by the company from an additional unit of production. Suppose that Company X can produce eight widgets at a total cost of forty dollars and nine widgets at a cost of forty-five dollars. The additional cost the company incurs by increasing production from eight widgets to nine widgets is five dollars. Since marginal cost is defined as the additional cost for an additional unit of production, five dollars is the marginal cost Company X incurs by increasing its production from eight widgets to nine widgets.

MARGINAL COST IS
⟶ ADDITIONAL COST
⟶ INCURRED FROM AN
⟶ ADDITIONAL UNIT OF PRODUCTION

$$$

The Real World of Profit Maximization

*A*ssume you make cars. You produce a car and take it to the marketplace. As long as you can sell the car for more than it costs you to make it, you will sell it. In the technical language of profit maximization, one would say that you would bring the car to market as long as the marginal revenue from the sale of the car is greater than the marginal cost of producing the car.

In fact, you will continue to bring additional cars to the market until the revenue from the sale of the car is equal to the cost of producing the car (marginal revenue equals marginal cost). Once your cost exceeds your $$$

revenue (marginal revenue is less than marginal cost), you will no longer bring cars to the marketplace because you will lose money on these additional units.

The Behavior That Maximizes Profit

I define profit maximization in behavioral terms as the act of *producing the right kind and the right amount of the goods and services the consumer wants at the lowest possible cost.*

Businesses know they are *producing the right kind of goods and services* if consumers are willing to buy them. Let me emphasize again that businesses that produce goods and services illegally have no place in this discussion because they are performing criminal acts.

Businesses also know when they are *producing the right amount of goods and services*. It is that level of output where marginal revenue is equal to marginal cost, as previously discussed. To produce less would mean the company would not bring units to the marketplace that, when sold, would result in revenues

$$$

greater than the cost of producing them, and this kind of behavior is inefficient. To produce more would mean the company would bring units to the marketplace that, when sold, would result in revenues less than the cost of producing them, and this kind of behavior is also inefficient.

Producing at the lowest possible cost is probably the most recognizable tenet of business behavior. Lower costs give the company a competitive advantage in the marketplace. Higher costs put it at a competitive disadvantage and reduce its ability to survive.

Profit Maximization and the Bottom Line

*T*he behavior of profit maximization as it relates to the bottom line will result in one of two outcomes. If the bottom line of the company shows a profit, it will be the most profit the company can receive *for using its resources efficiently*. If the bottom line of the company shows a loss, it will be the minimum loss the company can incur *by using its resources efficiently*.

The only thing the behavior of profit maximization will ever guarantee is the efficient use of scarce resources. When resources are allocated efficiently, we all have more of the things we want.

Profit Maximization and Ethics

hen businesspeople profit-maximize, that is, allocate scarce resources efficiently, people have more of the things they want, and that is good. When they do not profit-maximize, that is, allocate scarce resources inefficiently, people have less of the things they want, and that is bad. This is especially true if the things they want are food, health care, education, and other necessities of life.

Since ethics is basically the study of what is good and what is bad, then the decision to profit-maximize or not to profit-maximize becomes an ethical decision. Therefore, those resource allocators who try to use resources efficiently are ethical managers. Those resource allocators who do not try to use resources efficiently are not ethical managers.

There is more to profit maximization and ethics than the decision to use or not use resources efficiently. However, that discussion falls outside the scope of this book.

Profit Comparisons: One of the Least Important Uses of the Concept of Profit

*O*ne of the most distracting uses of the concept of profit in this country is our tendency to place too much emphasis on profit comparisons between companies or between industries. What does it mean to say that the oil industry makes more profit than the chemical industry? Usually, when this kind of discussion evolves, we talk about technical efficiencies, cost efficiencies, productivities, or differences in management. However, when all is said and done, when all of the technical analysis of profit is written and discussed, the bottom line is this: What does profit mean for the *community*? What does profit mean for *people*?

$$$

Afterword

rofit is an event, a happening. It happens because of a special kind of human behavior—the behavior of people producing the goods and services the community needs and wants.

By any measure, this kind of behavior constitutes the highest level of human activity and the highest level of social good. It is people engaged in the pursuit of profit who provide the goods and services the community needs and wants. I have never had my needs for food, clothing, shelter, or health care satisfied by people in the news media or in politics. Businesses, in the pursuit of profit, have satisfied these needs.

Profit is not a four-letter word. Its legitimate pursuit is the fuel for the engine that provides all the things we have. Profit also provides the incentive for us to use our scarce resources efficiently. The time has come to acknowledge what it is: *the most powerful concept ever developed for improving the quality of life for everyone, everywhere.*

Index

accounting profit, 27, 43–44, 63
Adam and Eve, 13–14
allocation of resources, 23–24, 69–70
alternative uses of resources, 47–48
art works, and profit, 10
attacks on profit, 49–50

benefits from pursuit of profit, 1–2, 52, 87–88
bottom line, 81–82
business, 3–4

capital, 26
comparisons of profit, 85
consumer demand, and profit, 11–12
cost(s)
  fixed, 29–30
  marginal, 71, 75, 77–78
  producing at lowest possible, 79–80
  in profit equation, 7–8, 27
  variable, 27, 31
  see also opportunity costs
creative skills, 26
cultural influences, on wants, 17–18

desire to consume, 15–16

Earth, preservation of, 67–68

$$$

economic profit, 27, 45–46, 63

efficient use of resources, 47–48, 70, 81–82

entrepreneurial skills, 26

ethics, and profit maximization, 83–84

event, profit as, 51–52, 59–60, 62, 87

farm, opportunity costs on, 35–38

fixed costs, 29–30

four horsemen of production, 25–26

Garden of Eden, 13–14

Gates, Bill, 52

government, 3–4

human achievement, and profit, 5–6

human behavior, and profit, 9–10, 53–54

illegally acquired profit, 55–58

infinite wants, 15–16

information, profit as, 11–12

Kamel, Raphael, on profit, 5–6

labor-time, 26, 31

land, 26

manufacturing, opportunity costs in, 39–40

marginal cost, 71, 75, 77–78

marginal revenue, 71, 73–74, 77–78
marketplace, 21
materials, and variable costs, 31
misconceptions about business, 65–66
more, as better than less, 19

needs, satisfying, 87–88

opportunity costs, 27–28, 33
    all costs as, 41–42
    and economic profit, 45–46
    on farm, 35–38
    in manufacturing, 39–40
    and preservation of Earth, 67–68
ownership, 21

people activities, 10
Perot, Ross, 52
planning, and opportunity costs, 37–38
political attacks on profit, 49–50
private enterprise, 21
private sector, 3–4
production, four horsemen of, 25–26
profiteering, 55, 56
profit maximization, 63–64
    and behavior, 69–70
    behavioral definition of, 79–80
    and bottom line, 81–82
    and ethics, 83–84
    and marginal cost/revenue, 77–78

$$$

technical definition of, 71
public sector, 3–4

resources
    allocation of, 23–24, 69–70
    alternative uses for, 47–48
    efficient use of, 81–82
    four basic, 25–26
    and opportunity costs, 33, 41–42
    scarce, 13–14
revenue, marginal, 71, 73–74, 77–78

skills, entrepreneurial/creative, 26
social good, and profit, 5–6, 9–10
socialism, 21, 24
status, 17–18
sunk costs, 30

technical definition of profit, 7–8
total cost, 27

variable costs, 27, 31

wants
    infinite, 15–16
    satisfying, 17–18, 87–88